# It Is Time

*A Series of Writings About What Time Has Come*

MARIE RENSHAW

PAGE PUBLISHING, INC.
New York, NY

First originally published by Page Publishing, Inc. 2019

ISBN 978-1-64584-893-6 (Paperback)
ISBN 978-1-64584-894-3 (Digital)

Printed in the United States of America

# It Is Time... We Help with True Success

What are we doing? And why are we doing it? Who do we think we are? What exactly are we trying to accomplish?

Do we ever ask ourselves why many times we find ourselves only being elevated by climbing the backs of another person? That is, we so desperately seek to rise out of whatever situation we are in, climb whatever ladder it is before us, accomplish whatever goal it is that our minuscule, little mind has decided was worth the very value of another; that regardless of what it may cost another individual, we must reach the top. But the top of what?

What is it that has us so eager to be at the top that we will demolish even the life of another to be there? Why is it that when we decide that "nothing will stop us"—that is exactly what we mean? Another person's reputation, character, integrity, and overall health and well-being are open to complete annihilation when it comes to us reaching our goal. That is, what we have set our minds on becoming has now become the very justification for complete assassination of anyone who even remotely thinks of hindering our advancement.

Why has it, for so very long, been drilled into our minds that one is only seen as successful by the life they live and the accomplishments they have made, while we never question the means they took along that journey to accomplish the goal? For one cannot reach the top when there is never truly a top to reach in the first place. Sadly, for many, the only thing they are on top of is the piled-up bodies of those whom they have slaughtered and dismembered along the way to get to where they desired to be.

*It is time…it is time* to see that the success we so desperately seek comes from within. That no amount of money, no job title, no career advancement, and no title we may wear on a badge or a series of letters we may see behind our name can truly dictate or define the person we are or the level of success we may have. It is time we realize that instead of climbing on the backs of our counterparts as a means to outdo them, we extend whatever help they may need so that they may stand strong and upright with their reputation, their character, their integrity, and their overall health and well-being completely intact and unblemished despite of the exceedingly brutal and controversial attacks formulated and carried out by another's greed.

It is time we become an encouragement—a source of uplifting and inspiration to one another the way God intended. That is, we sacrifice, in a manner, knowing that we are all part of something greater than ourselves. It is time that we no longer be so very eager to demolish one another so that we may be on top, but rather that we may willingly and unselfishly lay down our lives for another so that they may truly live. It is time we cease the war on one another to advance in a race that will never end and realize that in peace, humility, and love abounds hope and prosperity for not only ourselves but for all those around us. It is time that the selfishness and greediness of not only a person but a civilization ends so that real life, real prosperity, and real success can begin. It is time we realize that success and victory of one can be life-changing, but success and victory of many can be world-changing. It is time we stop competing with one another and begin in helping complete one another.

# It Is Time...to Wake and Forgive

Why? Why is it that at every moment in our lives when we have the opportunity to heal ourselves and reconcile with another from a past incident or episode, we would rather run like an Olympic track star in the complete opposite direction and act as if we were better than to be bothered by anything that happened previously in our lives; that we have no time to revisit our past because we have made it since then?

Why is it that when a situation offended, hurt, or deeply wounded us, we would rather stand up straight and walk away, never looking at the face of the one who hurt us, or even worse, face the one whom we've hurt and were hurt by our actions? Instead, we walk through our lives constantly digesting the guilt and anguish that may rise on occasion to remind us of an unresolved issue from our past.

Why is it that we would rather make up an excuse as to why we may have or may have not done something, may or may not have been somewhere, may or may not have known someone, and may or may not have taken part in something? Why is it that we think and feel that we are so perfect in this world that the audacity for an imperfect person to strike across our paths with a situation or action that we know could and should not have been done to or for us is unacceptable? Why is it that we feel the need and, most importantly, have the desire to not just have them feel hurt, but make them suffer? That in our totally unacknowledged way, we, at times, hope they feel the pain that they caused us at a time when we definitely did not deserve it. I mean, after all, did they not realize who we were and just how fortunate they were to have us in their lives? Didn't they know that in merely knowing and associating with us and in simply sharing time with us, their otherwise miniscule lives were given meaning? How dare they ungratefully take the opportunity they had in knowing such a person like ourselves and immaturely and irresponsibly take advantage and mistreat us? Exactly who do they think they are?

*It is time*…it is time for us to realize that we are all imperfect beings walking our journeys in an imperfect, chaotic world. It is time we realize it is not above or beneath anyone including ourselves to make mistakes and with or without the intent to hurt another's feelings. It is time we must realize that holding on to anger, animosity, pain, bitterness, and rage from being hurt by another only hurts the one who cages those feelings, and with every ounce of strength keeps them in captivity so that no one may ever know who they truly are. It is time that the pretend lives end and the real ones begin as we forgive our past actions and the past actions of others and realize life is given for living; it is not made for regretting. It is time we realize that in carrying the burden of guilt or hurt, one may never truly live the life they were created to live. It is time we realize the past can only dictate our future if we allow it, and that with each new day, new opportunity is created. It is time we no longer allow the past actions or mistakes of an individual to be a lifelong sentence we carry with us. It does not matter whether they may or may not make the change or whether we see ourselves as too good and them as unworthy for forgiveness, everyone, even the person who gave us the most pain, deserves forgiveness. It is time to let go of the pains of the past—be them given or received—and realize that we woke with the opportunity to not only live another day but to forgive another day.

# It Is Time...to Love Like a Child

As we walk down a street, an alley, a strip at the mall, or even an aisle at the local grocery store, why is it that when we see someone in need, especially a child, we turn our heads as though we did not see anything at all? How is it that we have reached a time in our existence that whenever we see a child in need, we turn away as if it is not our responsibility; and when we do help we do it speedily as though the inconvenience would just be too much.

How is it that in a world with so much products available, we can pass by someone who is in need? I mean, do we actually feel in our hearts that a child in a situation resulting in a developed need is just something we do not want to involve ourselves in? How have we entered into an era where if the need is not a physical need, we can just offer a band-aid solution with a few donated dollars? How have we decided to turn away and allow the child to attempt to survive in an unjust, unfair, disadvantaged, and chaotic whirlwind, hoping that someone may throw them a lifeline, but why can't it be just us who helps? How do we have the gall to justify the neglect we ourselves show to an innocent child as we stand by and witness them struggle through turmoil, which they themselves have no idea of how to escape? Why is it that many times we will knowingly avoid a conversation that could lead a child to a resolution of their life problems because we ourselves refuse to exchange our peace for their chaos? So we may rest peacefully in our comfortable beds at night after watching our favorite programs or completing our nightly routine surrounded by the ones we love, we avoid any and all interaction with the needy child we hurriedly ran away from that day? And most importantly, why are we okay with that?

*It is time...*it is time that when we see a child suffering, we come out of our safe and secure life and become a genuinely sincere line of help that they can openly and willingly take hold of without any feelings of judgment or bias against them. It is time we extend our arm and reach out our hand in such an inviting way that they will feel peace and hope at first touch. It is time we lay down our arrogance and our pride and we become a sincere and vulnerable cushion that a child may fall upon as they collapse from the weight of the burdens their little bodies have tried so hard to carry themselves.

It is time we allow ourselves to become a vessel used to cast light upon the children in even the most-darkened situations and show them that their darkness is not only seen, but it can be overcome. It is time we realize that a child's future is our future as well, and if we are not willing to extend ourselves to help them escape or resolve a detrimental situation they are in, we may also find ourselves in that situation as they become adults, which could impact our very lives. It is time we do all we can, even exhausting ourselves, to afford a child a life of peace, love, hope, and stability and ensure that they are nurtured and taught in the way they should go. It is time we realize that a child is just as much a significant and purposeful being as who we may see as the most powerful and prestigious person in all the world. It is time we realize that without a lifeline that very child may not become the very person God intended him or her to become and the ramifications of such could be world-changing, for we do not know what a child is destined to become unless we do everything in our ability to ensure they become exactly who they were created to be. It is time we must realize that children—be it our own or of strangers—are our future, and to think otherwise would be our own foolish self-deception. It is time we see all children as our children, and to be able to truly say we love our child, we must love all like a child, openly, freely, and willingly.

# It Is Time...to Converse

Do we realize that we are just a mere vessel that transfers either life or death upon every single being we come in contact with? Do we realize that in a conversation, regardless of its length, we either promote growth or we do not? Does one realize that even the briefest, innocent, nonchalant conversation can possibly leave an individual with an impact of either a positive or negative repercussion? Do we realize this? And more importantly, do we even care? When engaging with another individual, whether planned and intentional or random and spur of the moment, do we realize that each encounter we have can leave an impression? Do the words we speak hold value and have meaning, or are they just short and stifling, letting the recipient know that they are as meaningless as the conversation they were just engaged in? Do we actually take time to speak and converse, or do we just speak to take up time?

*It is time*...it is time we begin to talk to one another to promote growth and bring about life with each and every conversation we have. It is time we truly converse with one another, taking time from our busy lives and truly engaging in conversations that are positive, productive, and meaningful. It is time that our words carry weight, and when we ask another individual "how are you" it is time we show really genuine concern and actually mean what we say and not only speak the words but hear and listen to their reply. It is time we engage in conversation that will promote growth in each party involved, bringing about not only growth but the much-needed change so many are currently seeking. It is time we sit and open our minds, our hearts, and open our time to share thoughts, goals, opinions, and dreams with one another. It is time that when we ask our neighbors how they are doing, we actually speak in a genuinely sincere, compassionate manner, which allows them to feel an invitation to share and express with us. It is time that real conversations take place where we not only speak but listen. And when listening, it is not only to hear when they are done so that we may reply, but it is to truly open the doors that have for too long been shut. It is time we no longer speak to someone; it is time we talk with them. And in talking with them, we bring about an opportunity to open a door to gain wisdom and knowledge that we may never have known another individual had. It is time we no longer speak with either repetition or hesitation, and instead, we decide to open ourselves up to real conversation. It is time to not only speak but also to converse and *listen*!

# IT IS TIME... WE BECOME AWARE OF OUR WORDS

Do we even realize that with each and every encounter we have with one another, we either bring forth life or bring forth death? Do we realize that with each interaction we have with one another, we can either inspire growth or help bring about destruction? With each and every single encounter, be it big or small, we can lift and encourage, or we can help shove someone in the direction of defeat. When we speak to anyone, be it a loved one or a stranger, the very encounter that we are engaged in with them can hold a lasting impact that may have unforeseen, detrimental repercussions, which we may never know we had the responsibility of partaking in. In a few words, we could have replaced the very inspiration and encouragement one was seeking and longing for with greater fear and despair. Do we not realize that when we are engaged in conversation with someone, that during that engagement, they are receiving exactly what we are putting out toward them? With their longing for direction and hope to take a step in the right direction, we may have hastily guided them into an even further and more powerful downward spiral that they now may truly feel they have no means of escape? Do we consider that in what we may see as a simple conversation, the receiver may be at a point in their lives when all they are seeking is someone to give them those few words of encouragement to turn things around? I mean, do we ever consider that the words we let simply fly off the end of our tongue may hold power to completely change another's life? I mean, do we ever take the time to think about the possibility that we may have actually or could futuristically be the very reason someone either turned it around or gave up? Are we so caught up in our own lives that we just say whatever may come to our minds without thinking the possible lasting and powerful impact it could have on someone? Do we consider the damage we could possibly be doing to another? And more importantly, do we care?

*It is time*...it is time we conscientiously consider what we allow to roll off our tongue in any and all conversations we may have. It is time we hold ourselves responsible and accountable for the life and death we bring about in what we may see as just simple, miniscule little conversations we have with one another. It is time we literally think before we speak, knowing that there is power in the words we say to another, realizing that we *are* responsible for the outcome of another person's life—that is, we can literally bring about either growth or destruction in their lives with the words we spoke. It is time we engage wholly with one another in our conversations—knowing that with each and every conversation we may have, it is not mere words being said, but it is words that can bring about change. It is time we realize the power of the words we speak to another, and so when we speak, we consider whether the recipient is either filled with hope and conviction, encouraging them in the way they should go, or filled with despair and defeat, and we are responsible. It is time we lay our pride aside and realize that we may have fallen short with the knowledge needed, but we can always encourage another simply by allowing them to know that we are there for them, and although many of us may casually say that to so many people, *it is time* we truly be there! *It is time* to no longer say mere words, but *it is time* we speak and then stand behind the very words we say!

# It Is Time...to make a Deposit

Why is it that we expect to gain or receive something from someone that we have never instilled or placed in them? Why is it that we feel that an individual should be able to give us something when we have never given it to them? And at times when they do have even the smallest amount of something, why do we demand for them to have an unlimited surplus of it for us to use at our disposal, whether we deserve it or not? When it comes to trust, honesty, respect, virtue, and integrity, why is it that we demand from someone to show or give them to us? If they do not have them readily available, we become outraged? Yes, a person should show, give, and walk with these characteristics, but if those characteristics were not given, instilled, placed, or shown to an individual, who are we—with our imperfect selves—to demand the very quality someone may lack. And they may lack by no fault of their own. But even in knowing that an individual may be lacking in a specific area, which many may demand them to have, we still begin to at times demean and degrade the person for not having character. Yet do we have the character ourselves when we place demands on an individual who we clearly know cannot meet them?

Who exactly do we think we are when we stereotype, accuse, and label a person based on what they may lack when we ourselves do not know the very reason one may not have these very qualities? If one has never been shown respect, how can we honestly demand respect from them? If one has been mistreated and taken advantage of throughout their lives, how can we expect them to trust? If we do not explain to an individual what is meant by *virtue* and *integrity*, or better yet, if we are not a definitive example of exactly what those words mean, how can we expect someone else to walk in them? And with honesty, if an individual, especially a younger person, has fear of being honest because of repercussions, and has no idea what *integrity* is, how can we hold him or her to standards, which to and for them currently are unreachable? If we look at the lives of individuals like a bank account, for a moment, maybe we would understand that we cannot expect to withdraw what is not in there. And as with an account, if you overdraw, it will be in the *negative*, and there will be *penalties* for the overdraft! And before the thought would cross our minds that it's not our account, so it's not our problem, remember that *anyone* can make a *deposit*, but unfortunately, many only seem to want to withdraw!

*It is time*...it is time we begin to deposit in others what we or others may one day need to withdraw. It is time we instill and place in others what we ourselves and all those who encounter this person may benefit from. It is time we take the time to not just place a demand on someone to do as we expect, but we must begin to show another what exactly it is we are demanding from them. It is time to place and instill in others the characters and qualities that we know a family, a community, a society, and even a nation can and will benefit from. It is time we lose our expectations of people having specific qualities, and we approach those people with the very qualities we demand, whether they have them or not. It is time we show character, integrity, honesty, respect, virtue, and trust toward one another. It is time we drop the facade that is so deeply covered in our own self-righteousness and arrogance and begin to walk humbly in the very qualities we were made to show and reflect to and upon one another. It is time we refrain from lashing out when we are disrespected, and we reply with respect anyways because we are true to who we are and the qualities we have had instilled in us. It is time that, regardless of who they are, we *deposit* things in them that they will benefit from throughout their entire lives. And one will always remember who made a deposit when they were in the *negative*. It is time we take into account one's balance in these qualities before we begin to demand they be shown. It is time we stop demanding what one does not have to give because it was never placed in them. In doing so, we will always ensure that the complete balance will be a peaceful one. That peace will always lead to maturity and growth for both parties involved. It is time we no longer expect from others, and we begin to reflect to others. We must remember that in order to withdraw, one must first make a *deposit*!

# It Is Time...to Realign

How many times do we do something that we later feel regret for? How many times do we say something that we later realize was not at all what we would have usually said? And what about the times that our reaction is so completely different from what it should have been? How often do we complete an entire day without feeling even the slightest hint of guilt because we know we did or said something that we just did not mean to say or do? How many times do we act in a way that is more a reflection of our surroundings and our daily activities rather than a reflection of who we really are?

Do we ever wonder why we have begun acting in a way in which we know is not a part of who we are but rather is a result of who we have become? How many times do we reflect on how we are living and if we are living the way we once intended? And if we do reflect on whether we are living with a difference between the two, why is it that during the time we reflect on things, we feel a sadness? When we consider what we are actually doing and how we are actually living in comparison to what we set out to do and who we once desired to be, do we ever make the necessary changes to once again align with our purpose to fulfill the very purpose we were created for? Or do we just muster up the courage to go on since we have already strayed so very far from who we know we truly are deep down inside? Is the sadness too much to bear that we would rather keep on living and existing as we are than to face the turmoil, traumas, hurts, losses, pains, and sufferings from the past that caused us to make a detour in the first place? Is it fair that when we occasionally are out of our character with another because we have strayed so far from who we really are that we lash out on another and say or do things that we would have never imagined ourselves doing or partaking in? Is it fair to those around us that they may not even know the real us? Because we have put on a facade for so long, we have now become entangled in who we falsely portray and who only we know we are? Is it fair to them? More importantly, is it fair to us?

*It is time*...it is time we reflect on who we are and what we have become. It is time we consciously and willingly and truly search ourselves for what we hold deep within us and remove any and everything that has taken us off not only the path we were intended to walk but also the one we were created for. It is time we seek, embrace, and live for the purpose we were created for. It is time we knowingly face the things we have begun doing as a result of the misalignment we currently walk in, and make the necessary changes to realign with our purpose. It is time we search within us and find that desire—that childlike, innocent longing we all hold deep within ourselves—and begin to walk in it. It is time we live our lives according to the characters we strongly hold and be no longer dictated by the surroundings we may currently find ourselves in. It is time we stand strong in who we are, who we were created to be, and by whom we were created, knowing that we are not a mere product of our circumstances. It is time we stand strong by what's within us and no longer be consumed by what's around and in front of us. It is time to be true to our purpose that was instilled within us when we were formed in the womb and begin to live life as it was intended and then and only then will we be at peace. It is time we reflect, knowing we have walked in the purpose the creator designed specifically for us, and so when at night we lay down to rest, we truly rest. It is time the guilt is removed from our lives as we begin to walk as the very person created to walk the path we are once again on. It is time to remove the layers of life that we have carried for years and begin to walk freely and openly no longer a victim to circumstance but as an overcomer the way God intended. It is time to walk *our path* and realign!

# It Is Time... We Engage with Our Children

Do we ever truly listen to what a child is saying? Do we ever engage with them in a way that they are truly open to say what they are holding within?

Why is it that we seem to think that if a child is wearing clean clothes, has a decent body weight, and can even cast a smile when necessary that we assume the child is being treated well? We believe that they are okay, and at times, if the clothes and shoes are above the standard deemed acceptable by society that they are really living well. Why do we so easily believe that a child who is well-dressed, well-behaved, and most importantly, well-mannered is in a good environment and just has a great home life. Do we actually relate a child's well-being to the condition of their clothes, the shoes they wear, and the diet they maintain? Are we foolish enough to think that a child who may be ideal-looking may not be suffering at all? Is it because we are that naive, or is it because we do not want to take on the possible burden of getting involved in something that we would rather not be part of? I mean, has society decided that a pair of two-hundred-dollar shoes dictates whether or not that child is being properly cared for, or again, we must ask, Do we just not want to get involved?

Why is it that we can drive down a street and see a needy-in-appearance child and be willing to stop our car in five o'clock traffic to give them the very last dime in our pocket, but when we see a distant, quiet, and withdrawn child standing alone by themselves at the park, we are so very quick to blame it all completely on their shyness. Of course, they must only not be talking because they were raised to not talk to strangers. Or even worse, why is it that when we see a child who is acting out, we are so eager to ask where their parents are. We will quickly see the misbehaving child and demand that their parents be informed. Do we ever consider that maybe it is the parents who caused that child to act out? Do we actually question what is it they are acting out of? Is it anger? Is it fear? Is it abuse? Is it pain? Do we ever consider that that child may be just waiting for the moment a person, an adult, anybody asks them "are you okay?" instead of hastily labeling them the bad kid?

Why is it that it has become so natural to only see what one portrays on the outside rather than engaging and seeing what and who they truly are? Is it that we truly don't see this as a problem, or is it that we just don't care to take on a possible burden?

*It is time*…it is time we stop just hearing and looking, and instead, we begin to listen and truly see. It is time we do not limit ourselves to just passing a buck to a hungry child and begin to lend an ear and even a hand to any child. It is time we engage with the children running up and down the streets of our community, our society, our nation, and not ask them where they are supposed to be but start asking, Why are you here? It is time that we stop asking, Who is your parent? but instead ask, How is your parent?

It is time we no longer look at a child and think all is well; it is time we ask if it is. And in doing so, it is time we not only be prepared for an answer we may not be expecting to hear but be willing to help if need be. It is time we not only look at our neighbors but check on our neighbors too. It is time we engage even the "bad" kids, opening a door for them that they have for too long, remained hidden behind. It is time we realize children are our future, and we begin to exhaust every ounce of our being to ensure that they all know the value they hold within this world. It is time we reach out to them not with a waving hand but with a helping one, ensuring that the ones we encounter know that we are here. It is time that the adults of this world realize that the children may be hurting even though their pockets are not; that the bank accounts of their household may be large, but the amount of peace, stability, and love is in the negative. It is time that in realizing children are the future of this world, we must know and take responsibility in knowing that the condition in which we leave them is the condition we will someday find ourselves in. It is time we realize, as an adult person in this world, that we have a responsibility to the children of this world regardless of the vessel they were brought in by. Blood nor DNA does not exempt us from having a responsibility to our children. It is time we stop looking at the outside of a child and begin to engage and encounter the soul of a child. It is time we look at the children as life and fearlessly question if they are walking in death.

# It Is Time... They Know

As he sits in fear, shaking, does he truly know you are there? As he trembles with each and every step he takes, does he know that you would help him up if he were to fall or patiently lead him back if he were to go astray? As he becomes overwhelmed by the thought of failing, does he know that you see him as accomplished just by making it through all he has? As he takes a deep breath in and begins to hold it so as not to lose even a minute particle of what little he has left within him, does he know that you are there to help him restore, replenish, and grow?

When he stares off into space with a blank look, as though he is physically present but his mind has long since left and is taking part in a journey far from his current situation, does he know you see him, truly see who he is? As he looks around in complete confusion, wondering what it is that he is supposed to do, does he know that you are there to help guide and assist him in the way he should go? As he cowers down and his head becomes lower with the shrugging of his shoulders and the shrinking into a state of invisibility of his appearance, does he know you see him and you are there to uplift, build, and encourage him? As he either walks hastily or drags as if each foot holds the weight of a dump truck, does he know that you are there to walk with him and help support him each and every single step? As he scans a room and grimaces at all the happiness and joy he sees in others, does he know you are there to ensure that he one day feels and experiences that same happiness and joy? As he shrugs at the thought of even moving forward, does he know you are there to give him newfound strength? As he sits quietly, questioning whether or not to take part in a conversation as not to embarrass himself or others, does he know that he can turn to, rely on, and pull from the knowledge you hold? As he grows tired of living each day questioning who he is, does he know that you are there to guide, support, and encourage in all ways so that he may seek, find, embrace, and live the life and purpose he was specifically created for? As he wonders, day in and day out, of his value in this world, does he know that you would lay down your own life so that he may truly live? And as he sheds a tear questioning his worth in this world, does he know that your heart has a beat within for him?

*It is time*…it is time we hold the hands of children and let them know they are seen. It is time we sit with children and let them know that not only do we want to listen but that they themselves deserve to be heard. It is time we reach out to children and allow them to fall back on and rest in the knowledge we have, knowing that they can grow off and from it. It is time we allow children to see that they are cherished and that each breath they take should no longer be taken in fear or confusion but in peace and with a sound mind. It is time we stand strong for children and let them know that we too will face what they face and we will get through any and all obstacles together. It is time we let children know that our heart not only beats so we may live; it beats so that they too shall live. It is time we embrace children and let them know that the entire world would be different if they were not created as they were designed specifically for a purpose that no other individual in this world can perform as they are not them. It is time we reach out to children, take their hands, and stride alongside them with each new step in their life, letting them know that in their heaviest, darkest, most-burdened days, we will not only walk with them but will carry them in a time of weakness. It is time we look in the faces of children and let them know that they are a reason for our living. It is time we allow children to know that they no longer have to feel lost, and that without them, our entire future would be lost. It is time we help children, exhausting all our efforts, for them to become the very thing God intended. It is time we see children, and they KNOW!!

# It Is Time...to Stop Ignoring and Begin Restoring

Why is it for so long now that the majority of society sees life as meaningless or invaluable? Why is it that we are so eager to bring negativity and animosity that we no longer take a moment to consider the repercussions of our actions? Why is it that we have now become a society that feels it is better to end a life than it is to possibly end what we see as a potential problem?

When we drive down a street and see a situation arising, why is it that we press our foot a little bit harder on the gas as to hurry up and speed past, thinking of how grateful we are that we are not involved? We seemingly blow right past a situation that could possibly result in an individual's death, and in days ahead, we will make sure to comment on how we made it out of there just in the nick of time? When we see a situation arising, when we see a group of youth walking down the street in a group either large or small, why do we feel that the only thing we need to do is escape the threat of a potential catastrophe? Do we ever consider for a moment if we see a few youths about to enter into a conflict that we may be the only opportunity for peace to be brought into that particular situation? Or when we see the angry young man walking down the street, why is it that we can be in a vehicle with five passengers and still feel like we could potentially be in harm's way if we stopped and asked if he is okay? Instead, we will converse with our companions discussing what or who the young man we saw was about to confront. What has happened to the time and era when people took notice of their surroundings and then took action? Instead, we have traded those days for the days of ignoring our surroundings. Why is it that we will ignore what we see that's about to possibly ignite, yet we hastily go to social media or the lunch room at work the following day and speak so boldly and even proudly about what we witnessed about to happen? Yet instead, we decided to remove ourselves and let things just play out. Why do we ignore, and why is it okay? And why are we proud of the fact we chose not to get involved when any and all people on the face of this earth are loved by someone and their life matters

*It is time*…it is time we no longer cower down and run from a situation we see about to arise and we step in and attempt to diffuse and de-escalate it. It is time we not only take into consideration our own lives and remove them from a possible catastrophe, but it is time we take into consideration the lives of those caught in a moment of chaos and speak in peace, speak in value, speak in life. It is time we recognize each and every breathing person walking the face of this world has a purpose, and they were created for a reason specifically designed for them and that their purpose may promote life and growth in us all. It is time we walk in the peace we hold within and let our light shine upon the darkest situation so that warmth may be brought to the coldest moment, light shall be brought to the darkest hour, and peace may be brought to the most chaotic situation. It is time we open our eyes, see our surroundings, and cease ignoring what could be detrimental to a person's life, but involve ourselves in a way that stops the very violence about to take place. It is time we all realize that darkness is only the absent of light and we decide to commit ourselves to allowing the living, breathing light of life we hold within us to shine upon any and all situations we encounter and we begin to spread hope, peace, encouragement, and love, allowing them to see that someone stands strong for them and that they have worth. It is time we begin to walk in life even when we face death. It is time to stop ignoring and begin restoring!

# It Is Time...to End the Silence

What is it that has taken place over the last decades to have basically shut down communication among people? When was a vise placed upon the mouth of society so that conversation could no longer take place widespread and globally or even between neighbors? When were the jaws of society clamped so tightly shut that the only afforded gift for an individual is to breathe because they are no longer able to open their mouths and speak? How is it that we have entered into an era where we see wrongdoings and have become so stagnant in our ability to fight for what is right that we sit idly by and allow the monstrosities that we witness become root for casual dinner talk. We only speak about them, but never actually speak on the situation.

Why is it that in a chaotic, dark, death-encased world today, many choose to stand as frozen fixtures rather than speak up, speak for, and even, speak against the negativities that surround each and every one of us? Why is it that as a cemented wall of statues, we stand in complete alignment, questioning if and when one will step forward? Why is it we wait for another and have already made a definitive decision that someone will come, someone will speak up, someone will stand up, yet that someone cannot and will not be us? Why are we committed to being bystanders of darkness and turmoil rather than be activists of peace, hope, joy, love, growth, and most of all, *change*!

Why are we waiting for someone when that someone could and should be us? Maybe everyone whom we are waiting for is actually waiting for us!

*It is time*...it is time we no longer bite our tongues and remain silent, but instead, we must begin to speak up, for and even against the daily wrongdoings we see going on in our communities, our cities, our states, our nation, and even our world. It is time we speak up on the daily situations we encounter that are bringing and promoting negativity, hate, and violence, and we begin to provide positivity and solution with peace, hope, calmness, and encouragement. It is time we no longer look to our sides in a hope that someone will fall out of our statured alignment to stand up and for, but we ourselves make a committed decision to move forward and bring *change* to the world around us. It is time we no longer just see and sit idly; it is time we see and speak forth, step forward, and *rise up*. For in doing so, we will not just simply change a current situation, we will begin a ripple effect that will rush across this nation and this world, like a raging tidal wave destroying and removing all the chaos, darkness, negativity, injustice, and death we currently see in the world today. It is time for our silent witness to be put to rest and the hopeful, strong, wise, loving, peace-bringing activist that resides within each of our souls steps up and begins to battle!

# It Is Time...to Dismantle the Generational Weapons

Have we ever taken a moment and considered exactly where we are in relation to where we once desired to be as a child? Do we ever wonder how we ended up here and doing this? Have we ever given thought to what we once feared and hated as a child to what we once desired and longed for?

Most of us have hated something so very badly as a child, how is it that most have become the very thing they hated as a child? How is it that many have become who they once hated? How is it that many have begun to do to another what they once would have given their own life to escape from? How is it that many now emulate as an adult the very thing that broke them as a child? And why is it that many do not only take part in something they have seen as so detrimental as a child, but that with most, they do not even recognize they are now doing them?

Do we not remember what it was like to walk through a door completely overwhelmed, wondering if it would be like an obstacle course to get to our room, and silently moving as if in slow motion to glide through the house weightlessly as to not draw attention to one-self while continuously hoping to go unnoticed? Do we not remember what the sheer fear felt like—a lightning bolt shot through our feet and upward through our spines—when our name was called out when spotted? Do we not remember what it was like to try with every ounce of our being to mutter out whatever words we could when asked a question, praying that we would answer correctly and quickly to avoid the opportunity for the already present rage to escalate to an even higher level? Do we not remember what it was like to inhale fear with every breath we took while awaiting the response of the one who was addressing us? As a child, we would begin to answer while physically preparing for what we knew was about to ensue.

How is it that what we swore we would one day escape from we have now become the very perpetrator of it? Why is it that we would place another in the very situation that we thought we would never survive? Why is it that the hands, words, and actions of another have seemingly taken over our hands, words, and actions? As a child, the one thing that attempted to destroy us has now become the very thing that we do to destroy others. Whether it was abuse, neglect, alcohol, drugs, etc., why would we dare take part in the very thing that took away our childhood and, in doing so, took the lives of our own children?

*It is time*…it is time we remember the death we felt upon us in our darkest days and begin to seek life, letting go of that death and the aging grip it has had on us for decades. It is time we put down the bottle we once hated because it is not helping us cope with our problems; it has only become a weapon against our children—the very same way it was once a weapon against us. It is time we stand in the face of what took away our childhood, claimed our innocence, and shattered our trust and our hope and refuse to let it affect our lives or the lives of our children any longer. It is time we realize it has no power over us as we are the adults now and no longer the victims of the hands of another, but we are now the ones with the hands.

It is time we refrain from destroying our children with the same weapons that were used to destroy us. It is time we stand and take hold of the weapon that attempted to destroy us and discard them and begin to live. It is time we realize that regardless of the situations, the words, the actions of anyone against us as a child, we are no longer subject to be a recipient of such detrimental destruction, but we are the very ones able and capable to end its terror and become a bearer of life. It is time that all the tools deemed so valuable in the detrimental and destructive patterns of our childhood be dis-armed, dismantled, and discarded as they no longer have any impact or power in or on our lives or the lives of our children. It is time we release the guilt of becoming what we once hated and break down with our children and let them know that we only did what we knew as a child, but together, we cannot only stand but we can start anew and seek life together, grow strong together, and more importantly, heal together. It is time a generation becomes strong and encouraged knowing that they may have begun in a dark place, but the days of darkness are over; the days of fear are over; the days of despair are over. As our children have cowered down in fear, we must drop to our knees with them, take their hand, rise together, and begin to walk in a whole new life together knowing that *it is time* to conquer and overcome the death that has suffocated so many for so long. It is time to let go and *grow*!

# It Is Time...to Come from the Surface

How is it that we are in a time when we no longer look with depth? How is it that we only see what is portrayed on the surface and feel that we have enough knowledge to make an educated decision about a person, thing, or situation? Why do we feel we can make an adequate analysis of anything by only looking at the surface rather than discarding the stereotype of what we see and delve within to see if we have been misled? We have all at one time or another heard the saying don't judge a book by its cover, exactly why do we? Why do we continuously make assumption after assumption about something or someone we know nothing about and rely only on something we might have heard solely based upon something another may have or have not seen? Why do we consistently categorize everything—from people to situations—when we have not spent a moment on or engaged in or with them?

Is it fair to say that each young boy of the age of twelve in this society is the same? Is it fair to say that young boys of twelve with both parents in the home are the same? Is it fair to say that all twelve-year-old boys with the same household number, both parents present in the home, both having the same ethnic background, and same household income—that given a situation—will act the same way; that both will have the same desired or undesired outcome due to their similarities? Is it fair to say that both boys, or all boys with those characteristics can be expected to act, walk, think, move, feel, and behave the exact, same way in any given situation? No, of course not!

Then why is it we feel the need to act, speak, respond, and live in a manner that does not require the depth of a person being known, only with his or her surface characteristics, and we have decided to judge accordingly the very worth of a person based on those miniscule, superficial facts? Why is it that we allow what we see on the outside to depict whether or not we will ever engage with the inside of a person? Is it because we just do not feel the need to take the time, rather it would be quicker to just group everyone as a whole in the particular shelf-style bins of society and hope that they all fit together; this also makes it so very much easier for us to make our own personal choices as to who and what to engage and who and what to discard.

*It is time*…it is time to open our eyes and truly see the things and people around us. It is time to stop hesitating to walk on the side of a street because of the group we see down the block. It is time we no longer lock our doors, sitting at a light, because of the complexion of the man in the car that pulls alongside us and also time for that same man to stop expecting us to. It is time to stop helping, speaking, and supporting just our "own kind" and realize we are all a part of this world, and we are all the same kind—mankind.

It is time we remove the stereotypes, remove the restrictions and the categorizations, let go of the hesitation because of the superficial things we see, and it is time we begin looking at the depth of a person. It is time to take off the superficial filters and encourage, love, engage with, share with *all* our neighbors. It is time to truly love our neighbor because he is our neighbor regardless of anything we may see. It is time to reach out our helping hands, refusing to draw them back because of the condition of the opposite hand being reached forth in return. It is time we begin to see the depth, character, and soul of a man rather than their superficial surface characteristics. It is time to blindly love our neighbor coming from the surface and going to the depths!

# It Is Time…for True Advancement

What has it come to when the very thought of giving away a dollar we have worked so hard for, or that we feel we have so rightfully earned, becomes equivalent to losing a limb or at times even our lives? Why is it that the thought of handing someone something that we have decided they did not earn has become a dreadful task that many will unfortunately choose to shy away from or boldly choose to ignore? What has become of us when we have decided it is more important for us to keep "our look" and "our appearance" to an acceptable level for an imaginary board of decision-makers who will decide if it is acceptable or not for us to even exist? Why is it that we ourselves will take each and every cent we have earned or laid claim to and use it to expand our land and our belongings and sometimes even the very number in our household so that we will fit into a place in society, which one must become a part of so that our lives are deemed acceptable?

Why is it that it is almost detrimental to our lives if we do not upgrade our lives, our families, our lands, and our belongings in the first breath of a financial growth? That is, if we are given an opportunity to advance financially, we immediately set out to advance everything we have so that literally the only advancement was materialistic and personal growth was non-existent. Why is it that we constantly seek the bigger and better for ourselves while at the same time another has nothing? That another living, breathing being can lay still and quiet on the street on a cold winter night, covered by only some used-up, dirty clothes, and in passing them, if we do not snarl at the audacity this very person has for lying so abruptly in our path, we become almost nauseated at them that we arrogantly decide whether or not this being, this person is even worth the dollar we may or may not have in our pocket? Why is it that we have so arrogantly decided whether they hold worth at all? Who exactly do we think we are that we have now become what we see as supreme ruler and decider if this person has a worth to them at all?

The pride and arrogance we display has become a deathly toxin laying claim to not only this life but the countless lives similar to this that we so repetitively have chosen to ignore during our day. Sadly, the worst part of that deadly toxin that is multiplying and spreading across the land to unknowing individuals and silently annihilating countless individuals is not only destroying their lives…it is destroying ours. We are dying at the spread of a deadly toxin that we do not even realize we are emitting.

*I*t is time...it is time we begin to advance our lives by the advancement of another. It is time we begin to see another in need and realize that our wants, dreams, and desires can no longer outweigh the needs of another. It is time we step down from the seat of judge, jury, and executioner and step into the role of partner, provider, and supporter. That is, for us not only think of ourselves as the only beneficiary of our hard-earned money, but that we seek out and find the needs of our friends, our neighbors, the stranger on the street, the person we saw the night before on our way home and realize that they not only have needs but are living, breathing beings that have a worth that far exceeds the mere few dollars that we may spare them. That is, their lives have a worth that cannot and must not be dictated by a few pieces of paper that one is willing to give.

It is time we cease from emitting a toxin that is devouring the lives of so many, and we must begin to walk as a willing vessel not only sharing our lives with another but giving all we have to ensure the life of another. It is time we lay to rest our own personal expansion every opportunity that we have and begin to promote and support the expansion of another. It is time that our growth comes from beyond the four walls we call home and realize that true expansion, true growth, true life cannot be held back or bound by the limits we attempt to place on it. It is time that our lives not only reflect the growth and advancement of ourselves but reflect the growth and advancement of our being, our community, and our civilization as a people. We must stop growing as individuals; *it is time* we grow as a *whole*.

# It Is Time...to Stop the Attack and Be the Resolution!

As we attempt to strike out on another with our anger and our animosity, what is it that we are determined to gain? Why is it that a negativity that persistently and uncontrollably grew throughout our day has now become a weapon for us to attack an unknowing and underserving individual with? Why is it that we have bottled up and caged a problem that only we knew existed and then forcefully shoved it into an innocent victim's lap? We have shifted it from us to them in a moment's time, expecting them to take ownership of something they did not even realize existed. From a mere encounter, they have become a victim of our hard day, of our personal trial, of our hardship. Without warning, they have become a recipient of the repercussions of something that they themselves had absolutely nothing to do with.

Why is it that, in a breath, we can change someone's whole demeanor, their entire day by throwing a backlash at them that they not only had no responsibility for but they themselves did not deserve to be struck down by? Who do we think we are to take our chaos and our problems and our bad day and leave them at the feet of another because we have chosen not to deal with them ourselves? That is, we take what was meant for our destruction, and we deflect it by giving it to another and destroying them.

Why is it we feel our problems are the responsibility of someone else? Did the person receiving the backlash deserve the assault they are taking because we held onto our bad thing all day, did not deal with it, and decided to let it go on whomever walked up at the time we decided to let it go? How is that right, and how is that fair? How is it that we cannot take ownership of a problem we are facing, but we can decide to randomly pick who shall be the bearer of our burdens when they are our problems, our chaos, our burdens?

*It is time* we do not allow a difficulty to become a disaster. It is time that when faced with a problem, we do just that. We face it, we own it, we solve it. It is time we walk in peace, knowing that with each and every encounter throughout the day, we do not meet it with the repercussions and backlash from prior events or situations. It is time we walk in peace, knowing that we were created to walk this world as an intricate part of its very existence. That is, we are to bring encouragement, uplift, and bring life to one another. It is time that when we look into another's eyes, we do not look through a jeopardized lens because of bottled-up emotions and feelings, but we look with a gentle heart and a loving soul and embrace each and every encounter we are involved in. It is time we no longer allow the events of a day to be the demise of another or allow it to dictate the way we continue throughout our day, our week, our lives. It is time we let go, have faith, and conquer as we were created to do. It is time we no longer allow the previous events of any situation affect the way we see what is before us. It is time we look forward and not back, knowing what happened previously is the past and not the present. It is time we see each and every encounter with another individual as an opportunity to share joy, peace, hope, and love. And in doing so, we may just provide that person with the very tools to not only solve a problem they face but find resolution on our own.

# ABOUT THE AUTHOR

Surrounded daily by the children of this world, the allowance has been made for the author to not only see the repercussions of society's choices and actions on people, but she has gained a unique perspective on how those very choices and actions have an effect on our future, the *children*. From her perspective, *it is time* we take a look at our lives and see how we can stop this ripple effect of negativity from further spreading across our communities, our cities, our nation, and even our world. *It is time* we search within ourselves and see what changes we can make to promote growth, unity, restoration, and healing, not just within our own lives but also to the lives of all whom we encounter.

CPSIA information can be obtained
at www.ICGtesting.com
Printed in the USA
BVHW030539101219
566193BV00001BA/88/P